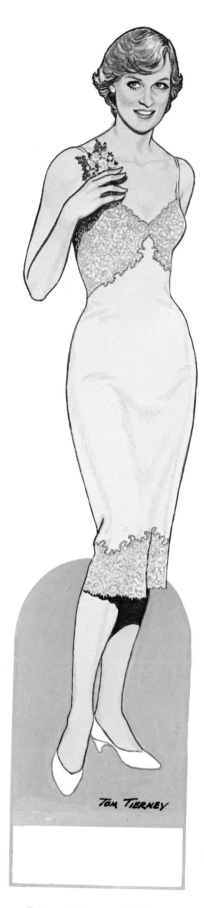

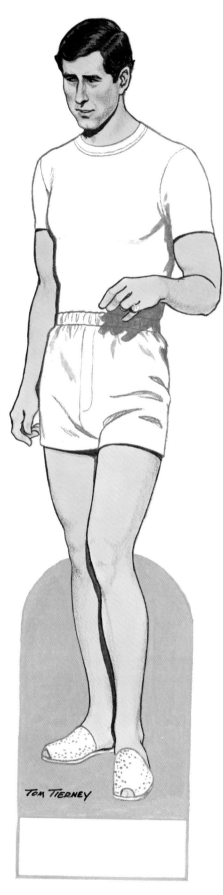

Diana, Princess of Wales.

Charles, Prince of Wales.

Plate 1

Wedding dress by David and Elizabeth Emanuel.

Plate 2

Bridesmaids' dresses by David and Elizabeth Emanuel;
page's uniform a replica of a uniform of 1863.

Naval dress uniform
worn at the wedding.

Plate 3

Going-away suit by Bellville Sassoon.

Dress by Donald Campbell, worn on the honeymoon.

Plate 4

Suit by Jaeger, first worn on a tour of Wales.

Sailor dress by Bellville Sassoon.

Plate 5

Plaid dress by Caroline Charles,
worn at the Royal Braemar Gathering.

Kilt and jacket.

Plate 6

Suit by Donald Campbell, worn in Wales.

Suit worn for the state visit of Queen Beatrix.

Plate 7

Suit worn on Christmas Day, 1983.   Suit worn on Christmas Day, 1983.

Plate 8

Sweater by Joanna Osborne and Sally Muir.   Country outfit with Inca sweater.

Plate 9

Russian-style winter outfit.

Coat of Welsh wool.

Plate 10

Evening dress by Bellville Sassoon.

Tuxedo for evening wear.

Plate 11

Dress worn at Royal Ascot.

With Prince William, in a suit by Jan Van Velden.

Plate 12

Evening dress by Bellville Sassoon.

Suit by Bruce Oldfield.

Plate 13

Evening gown by David and Elizabeth Emanuel.

Dress worn at the State Opening of Parliament.

Plate 14

Evening dress by Bruce Oldfield.

Evening dress by Jan Van Velden.

Plate 15

Suit worn for the
christening of Prince Henry.

Suit worn for the
christening of Prince Henry.

Plate 16